10-15

NO FUNNY BUSINESS

NO FUNNY BUSINESS

by EDITH THACHER HURD

Pictures by Clement Hurd

An I CAN READ Book

HARPER & ROW, PUBLISHERS

New York, Evanston, and London

"We will go on a picnic,"

said Father.

"A picnic?" said Mother.

"Yes," said Father.

"We will go on a picnic today."

"Oh good," said Brother.

"Oh good," said Sister.

"Oh good," barked Smart
the dog.

"What's so good about that?"

said Carl the cat.

"I won't go on a picnic."

Carl liked to say,

"I won't."

Then Mother, Father, Brother,

Sister and sometimes Smart,

said,

"Oh, Carl.

Please, Carl.

Please come on our picnic."

But today nobody said,

"Oh, Carl.

Please, Carl.

Please come on our picnic."

They forgot.

Mother just said,

"I am going to take something

good to eat."

Father said,

"I will take something

good to drink."

Brother said,

"I will take my ball."

Sister said,

"I will take my doll."

Smart said,

"What will I take?"

Carl did not know what to say

so he said,

"Cats do not go on picnics."

11

"All right," Mother said.

"You stay at home, Carl.

Take good care of the house."

"No funny business,"

said Father.

"No fooling around."

"Cats don't fool around,"

said Carl.

Away they all went in the car.

Carl stayed at home.

"What will I do?"

said Carl.

Carl walked in the garden.

The birds were away.

Carl walked in the kitchen.

The mice were not at home.

"I will go to sleep,"

said Carl.

"Then I will not fool around."

Carl went to sleep.

He went to sleep

in Father's big chair.

Z-Z-Z-Z-Z-zzzzzzzzzzzzzzzz

Sh! Sh! Sh!

Carl is asleep.

He is dreaming.

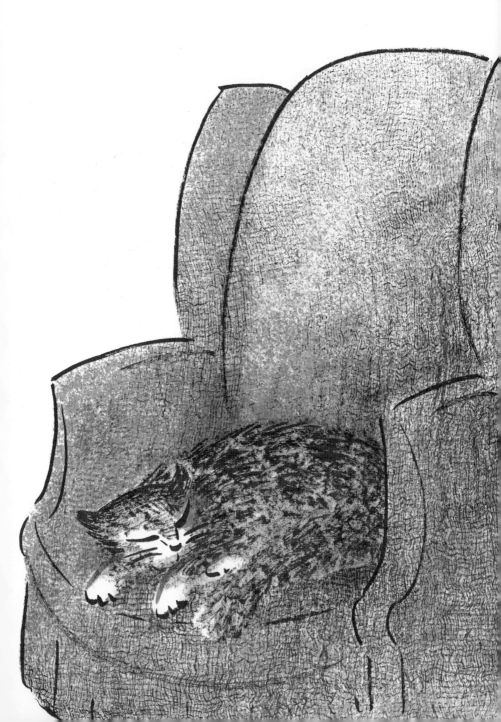

Carl is dreaming that

he is going on the picnic.

He is dreaming that

he is driving the car.

He is driving very fast.

"Don't drive so fast,"

said Father.

Sister said,

"Carl, don't drive so fast."

Mother said,

"Oh! Oh!"

Brother said,

"Drive faster, Carl."

Carl came to the top of the hill.

"Oh! Oh!" said Mother.

"Stop, Carl, stop!"

said Father.

But Carl did not stop.

Away they went.

21

A policeman stopped Carl.

"Cars must stay on the road,"

said the policeman.

"Why are you driving so fast, cat?"

"Cats like to drive fast,"

said Carl.

"You will get hurt,"

said the policeman.

"Cats never get hurt,"

said Carl.

"They have nine lives."

"No more funny business,"

said the policeman.

"No," said Carl.

"No more funny business."

Carl drove very slowly.

He drove to the beach.

"We will picnic here,"

said Father.

Carl stopped the car.

Everybody got out.

Carl made a fire.

"Don't make too big a fire, Carl,"
said Father.

"Fires make me warm and happy,"
said Carl.

"What will we cook
over this nice warm fire?"

"Hot dogs," said Mother.

"Good," said Carl.

"I like hot dogs better

than real dogs."

28

Smart barked at Carl.

But Carl was cooking a hot dog.

He did not say anything.

Carl ate one, two, three, four,
five, six, seven, eight, nine,
ten, eleven, twelve, thirteen,
fourteen, fifteen, sixteen,
seventeen, eighteen, nineteen,
TWENTY hot dogs.

"Stop," said Mother.

"You will be sick."

"Oh no," said Carl.

"Cats like to eat dogs."

"Woof," barked Smart the dog.

31

"Who wants to go swimming?"

said Father.

"I do," said Brother.

"I do," said Sister.

"I do," barked Smart.

"I will watch," said Mother.

So she watched.

Father swam.

Brother swam.

Sister swam.

Smart swam.

Mother watched.

"Where is Carl?"

said Father.

"Where is Carl?"

said Sister.

"Where is Carl?

Here, Carl. Here, Carl."

said Brother.

Mother had been watching.

But she had not seen Carl.

He was not in the tree.

He was not in the boat.

"Carl. Carl.

Where are you?"

said Sister.

"Perhaps he swam out too far,"

said Brother.

"Oh no," said Sister.

"Poor Carl. Poor little Carl."

Sister began to cry.

"Where are you, Carl?"

"Here I am," said Carl.

Sister looked.

Brother looked.

Mother and Father looked.

There was Carl.

Then he swam back.

"How did you get there?"

said Sister.

"I was watching," said Mother.

"But I did not see you."

"I swam under water,"

said Carl.

"It is late," said Mother.

"We must go home."

"Oh no," said Brother.

"I want to play ball with Smart."

"All right," said Mother.

"You can play ball with Smart

for a little while."

Smart and Brother played ball.

Smart did not play very well.

He could not catch the ball.

Carl caught the ball for Smart.

He caught the ball all the time.

Carl ran with the ball.

He won the game.

"I won the game,"

said Carl.

Smart did not like Carl to say

that he won the game.

"There is too much funny business

around here," said Father.

"We are going home."

"Oh no," said Sister.

"I want to go for a ride

in the boat.

I want to take my doll."

"You cannot go alone,"

said Father.

"You might fall in the water.

Your doll might fall in the water."

Carl jumped into the boat.

"I will take you," said Carl.

"Thank you," said Sister.

Carl rowed and rowed.

"Don't go out too far,"

said Mother.

Sister jumped up.

She waved to Mother.

Sister's doll almost fell

into the water.

Carl caught it.

"Come back. Come back,"
called Father.
"I want to row back,"
said Sister.

"No," said Carl.

"You do not know how to row."

Sister began to cry.

"Well, all right," said Carl.

Sister began to row.

She did not know how to row
very well.

"Oh dear! Oh dear!"

said Sister.

Mother was watching.

"Oh, oh," she said.

"Help! Help!

What will Carl and Sister do now?

They will be lost at sea.

Help! Help!"

Carl dove into the water.

He swam and swam.

"Oh thank you,"

said Sister.

"You saved my life, Carl."

"It's nothing, really," said Carl.

"There's too much funny business

around here," said Father.

"We are going home."

So they all went home.

When they got home

there was Carl.

He was curled up

in Father's big chair.

He was still dreaming

about the picnic.

"Sh-sh-sh-sh," said Mother.

"Carl is asleep.

Don't wake him up."

When Carl heard Mother say,

"Don't wake him up,"

he woke up.

"I was dreaming," he said.

"No funny business?"

said Father.

He looked around the room

to see if Carl had been

up to any funny business.

"No," said Carl.

"No funny business.

I have been dreaming.

I dreamt that I went on

YOUR picnic."

"Oh, Carl," said Sister.

"Poor little Carl.

Did you really want to go

on our picnic?"

"We will go again soon,"

said Mother. "Will you

come with us then, Carl?"

"Oh, Carl.

Please, Carl.

Please come on our picnic,"

said Mother, Father, Sister,

Brother and Smart.

"Please come on our picnic."

Carl didn't say,

"I won't."

He didn't say,

"I will."

He just said,

"Well, maybe."

But he was very, very happy.